MW00442537

This journal belongs to

_____

Introduction

This *Nature's Whispers* journal is your safe place. This is a place where you may focus your thoughts, feelings, wishes, and desires through writing. You can set goals, dream dreams or reminisce. You may even like to try looking at a situation from a different perspective. You may choose to write down ideas that you have, places you have been, people you are spending time with or phrases that inspire you. You might like to find a wonderful place outdoors where you can write your heart's desires. If you aren't able to go outside, perhaps you have a window that overlooks a favorite part of your garden or has a beautiful view of the outdoors.

There are no rules. You can write in full sentences. Or maybe you prefer bullet points. This is your journal and it's up to you to decide what you want it to look like. The purpose of your journal is fluid and ever-evolving – think of it as an extension of you that may grow and change with you, your moods and your aspirations.

You can write, sketch, draw, doodle, and use your imagination.

You may wish to use this journal to connect to your intuition or receive support from your guides or higher self. Reflect on the artwork and pay attention to any feelings that arise in you. Write them down. As you practice this, you may find you begin to receive deeper messages, insights or epiphanies about whatever it is that is currently occupying your thoughts.

Trust yourself and allow your thoughts and feelings to flow into this journal. Have a blessed experience!

– Angela Hartfield

Nature is filled with magic, imagination, opportunities,
possibilities, healing and adventure.

*Take Mother Nature's lead and give yourself the gift of connecting
with the ever-present wisdom of the outdoors.*

"Look deep into nature, and then you will understand everything better."
— *Albert Einstein*

Sit in nature and set clear intentions about what you wish for in life.

Nature asks that you allow for blessings to come into your life.

If you were given one wish, what would you wish for?

The clarity you desire is at hand.

Trust in yourself, and in your support from nature and the Divine.

Today, I choose to see the beauty in nature around me.

"Man's heart away from nature becomes hard."
— *Luther Standing Bear*

Take a deep breath of fresh air and regroup.
Don't feel the need to fight whatever is going on.

*Whatever you are experiencing now is a creation
that you have brought into existence.*

*Nature communicates with you through your physical
senses of sight, touch, smell, and sound.*

Notice how gracefully nature releases old or dying aspects of itself.

I am willing to let go and begin again with a clean slate.

Simply choosing to stay happy and sending that happiness
out from your heart will benefit those around you.

Nature shows me that I have a creative touch and the ability to generate new and wonderful things.

"Adopt the pace of nature: her secret is patience."
— Ralph Waldo Emerson

Just as seeds break through the surface of the earth,
you will have your emergence.

Nature makes blooming and growing look effortless,
but we sometimes forget that all the details — sun, soil, water,
air and nourishment — have been in place for some time.

Open your heart and let nature fill it with love.

I trust the process and let nature take its course.

The truth of our world, nature, and environment is love.

I allow love to flow into my heart.

The only limits I have are those that I impose on myself.

The positive energy that you radiate from your heart
while standing in nature will attract that which you desire.

Attune and align yourself with the rhythms of nature around you.

It is important to maintain peace in all areas of your life.

"Forget not that the earth delights to feel your bare feet and the winds long to play with your hair." — Khalil Gibran

Look to nature for small signs that situations,
desires and things are beginning to fall into place.

"The richness I achieve comes from nature, the source of my inspiration."
— Claude Monet

You are on a journey where you are coming to understand
your feelings and desires more clearly.

Take a break and enjoy a quiet period out in nature.

Nature's crystals are created deep within the earth.

Open your heart and allow love to bring you joy, serenity, renewed energy, passion, and unrelenting happiness.

Go deep within you to find treasures just as beautiful
as those that surround us in nature.

Open your heart and your reality to the immeasurable gifts from nature.

*I notice the miracles and blessings that show up in my life
in unexpected ways.*

Nature's loving energy surrounds you.

"Nature does not hurry, yet everything is accomplished."
— *Lao Tzu*

Nature is continually sending you subtle messages.

Nature is continually enticing us to spend time in her ambience.

Notice the new beginnings in nature all around you.

Live in the present and trust your own abilities.

Plant your seeds and willingly venture into new territory.

Just as trees shed their leaves, let go of whatever
no longer serves you in your life.

Focus on what is most important to you.

It's time to step out of the box and the old way of doing things.

Let nature inspire you to create magic in your world.

Create with the intention of filling your life with joy and happiness.

Take a minute to sit in nature and enjoy the wisdom of the trees.

"One touch of nature makes the whole world kin."
— _William Shakespeare_

*Get outdoors and allow the sunshine to kiss your face
and nature to touch your soul.*

*Nature asks you to look to the horizon and see that
your possibilities are endless.*

Just as a flower blossoms, allow yourself the opportunity to bloom.

Nature teaches me to enjoy and love who I am.

Nature contains the full array of the light spectrum.
This is the same light that shines out of every child while they are still in
touch with the magic of the world and nature.

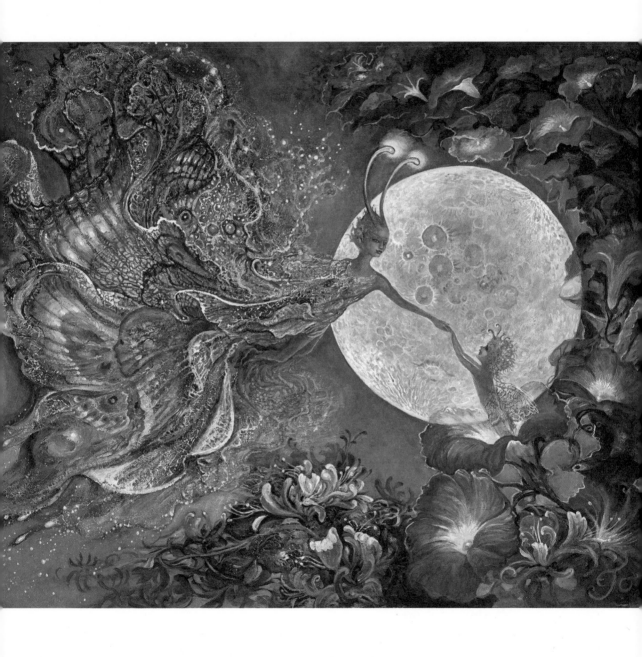

Mother Earth is continually showing me her abundant blessings.

Take time in nature to contemplate the things
that you enjoy most in your life.

Nature is whispering to you — choose to listen to its message.

Taking a walk out in nature is guaranteed to shift your energy.

*There is no feeling quite like having the wind blow through your hair
and the sun shine on your back.*

"I can enjoy society in a room; but out of doors, nature is company enough for me." — William Hazlitt

Nature is always there waiting patiently for you to take notice.

I take time for myself; breathing the fresh air that nature provides for me.

I am willing to engage with nature and live my life to the fullest.

*Just as spring comes at the perfect time, all is revealed
in the same space of perfection.*

When you are feeling overwhelmed, remember nature is there to assist you in recharging your energy.

I take some time each day to consciously connect with nature
in some small way.

Notice the season and the changes that are taking place out in nature.

Think about the clouds you see in the sky.
They are constantly moving, changing and reinventing themselves.

*Align your rhythm with the heartbeat of the earth
and slow down your emotions and thoughts.*

Find a place outdoors to sit and daydream
about what delights and inspires you.

Nature is the perfect representation of the harmony of opposites —
masculine and feminine.

Pay attention to signs along the way as nature works to assist you.

All of nature shows us the importance of creating a strong network.

"Climb up on some hill at sunrise. Everybody needs perspective once in a while, and you'll find it there." — *Robb Sagendorph*

Without a strong root system, the trees would simply topple over. Take time to reflect on your own support system and make adjustments if needed.

As I watch the harmony of nature,
I am willing to give and receive love.

*Stretch out under the night sky and consider the stars are equal
to the number of blessings in your life.*

The time for respect for life and all living things, for attuning to nature and to the creatures of the earth is at hand.

Nature is continually sharing its beauty for us to appreciate.

Beholding a rainbow is a gift. When you encounter a rainbow's beauty, it is the perfect time to be grateful for the gifts in your life.

*A waterfall represents the positive flow of thankfulness
that brings joy into your life.*

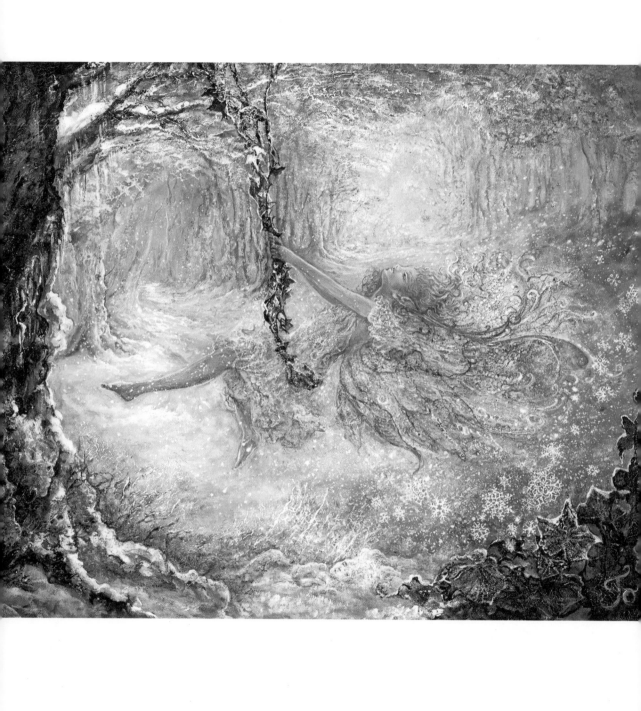

"To forget how to dig in the earth and tend the soil is to forget ourselves."
— *Mahatma Gandhi*

Nature is waiting to assist you to ease your stress
and generate feelings of goodwill and love.

Laughter is like a powerful wind that breaks up stagnant energy.

Nature's energy is filled with healing, progress and satisfaction.

Let worries or challenges from the past fade away as you focus on nature and the joy that surrounds you.

If you feel like your energy is low, infuse your mind with the warmth of sunlight and visualize this light bringing new energy to you.

Just as a river meanders, your life is constantly shifting and developing.

*Envision a tree. Look up high into its branches
and ask if there are any messages for you today.*

Sit in silence and listen to the sounds of nature.

"Reading about nature is fine, but if a person walks in the woods and listens carefully, he can learn more than what is in books, for they speak with the voice of God." — George Washington Carver

*Nature is filled with contradictions; beauty and danger, weak and strong.
It teaches the importance of balance.*

A tree trunk may bend and curve as it adapts to its surroundings,
yet it always stays true to its purpose.

Look at a tree stretching up into the sky and consider how
you can challenge yourself and stretch your limits.

Notice new growth in nature and see the potential
of all that is possible in your life.

In nature, it's easy to appreciate the interconnectedness of all things.
Take a moment to reflect on how this same interconnectedness
extends into the rich tapestry that is your life.

Nature's messengers are vast and come in many forms.

Take a moment to kick off your shoes and feel the cool grass under your feet.

*You have access to the infinite source of love and resources
provided by Mother Nature.*